The Gravity
of Flesh

Also by Jill Breckenridge

Civil Blood

How To Be Lucky

The Gravity of Flesh

poems

Jill Breckenridge

NODIN PRESS

Cover drawing copyright © 2009, R. W. Scholes,
all rights reserved.
Book design and layout, John Toren.

Library of Congress Cataloging-in-Publication Data

Breckenridge, Jill.
  The gravity of flesh / by Jill Breckenridge.
      p. cm.
  ISBN 978-1-932472-81-3
  1. Human body--Poetry. 2. Life--Poetry. I. Title.
  PS3552.R362G73 2009
  811'.54--dc22

                                        2009012424

Nodin Press, LLC
530 North Third Street
Suite 120
Minneapolis, MN
55401

www.nodinpress.com

again, for John Fenn

ACKNOWLEDGEMENTS

My deepest gratitude to the following publications and people:

Milkweed Chronicle, Vol. 2, No. 3, Fall 1981: "The Gravity of Flesh," seven poems of the twelve-poem sequence published under the titles "Food and Flesh," "Feathers and Flesh," "Judging Flesh," "Joined Flesh," "Fear and Flesh," "The Bond of Flesh," and "The Revelation of Flesh"

A View from The Loft: A Magazine for Readers and Writers, Vol. 25, No. 5, December 2001: "Contour Line Drawing"

Family Reunion: Poems about Parenting Grown Children, Chicory Blue Press, 2002: "Winter Heart"

For the lines from *Divisadero* © 2007, by Michael Ondaatje, I thank Michael and his publisher, Alfred A. Knopf.

Thanks are due to my five grown children for their ongoing support. Unflagging personal and writing encouragement also came from Phebe Hanson, Pat Francisco, Margaret Hasse, Jackson Petersburg, Joan Drury, Chris Porter, Todd Maitland, Dr. Keith Prussing, Carol Mockovak, members of my writers' book club, and my retreat group.

Many of these poems were written at Ragdale, a residence for artists in Lake Forest, Illinois; and at the North Shore of Lake Superior, in the rented cottage of Joan Drury. Without quiet places to think and write, many of these poems would not have been written.

My gratitude to the doctors and nurses at Mayo Clinic and Virginia Piper Cancer Institute who helped me during the eight challenging years I fought to reclaim my life. Special thanks go to Dr. Kenneth Cherry, an inspired vascular surgeon.

Finally, working with Nodin Press publisher, Norton Stillman; bookmaker, John Toren; and artist, Randy Scholes has been as pleasurable a partnership as I could imagine.

I am grateful to be alive in this world with so many large-hearted people.

CONTENTS

The Gravity
of Flesh

There is the hidden presence of others in us, even those we have known briefly. We contain them for the rest of our lives, at every border that we cross.

– Michael Ondaatje
Divisadero

I

Evolution

When I'm Ready To Begin

life in this world, Mother, hair
coal-black and bobbed, isn't ready,
thinks sex is a terrible bore.

Father's her gangster, she's his moll
in the Portland bar they manage. People
drive miles to watch them—like a movie.

Her slender body sways as she sashays
guests to their tables through smoky clouds,
shining glass, and thundering words.

It's 1938 and no one thinks of Europe
or the little man who marches penguin-
style, *Sieg Heil!* so they order another

beer, down it with a chaser, order
dry martinis, Scotch on the Rocks,
cup their best friend, Jack Daniels,

Cutty Sark, or Tanqueray—even Jim Beam—
and to dull the ache next day, it's back
in for hair of the dog, hair of the dog.

My father meets with business partners
who wear dark glasses, shiny suits, enter
through the back door, and never

pay for drinks. I'm skating around
water rings on the table, wanting
to be born, waiting to be born,

but my father is too busy, so I find
Mother at the cash register, whisper,
Is this the time? and she says,

No, not now, and even as a baby
wanting to be made, I know she means,
No, not ever, and I despair, though I'm

unable to cry, made of light and air
and promise, and just as I'm about
to give up, my favorite grandmother dies.

She's the determined one, the one they say
I'm like. When she's sixteen, living
at home on the Idaho sheep ranch, her

parents send her out to find her brother
because he's late for dinner again,
and even though she doesn't want to,

she rides her horse through sagebrush
and the startled high jinks of jackrabbits.
Watching for rattlers, she takes the top

of the ridge until she sees a rider
below, and she's so mad, she spurs
her roan off the ridge and gallops

down stiff-legged, dirt and lava rock
flying, and as she gets close, yells,
Where the hell have you been?!

then reins in when she sees that he's
a stranger—the man she'll soon marry—
my grandfather, and she'll have four kids,

which nearly kills her, but they'll all
go to college on her egg money, except
my father, who insists on going to jail,

and she calls out to me, *Is that you, Jill?*
Where the hell have you been?! and the day
she rides out of the picture, I ride in.

EVOLUTION AND BIRTH TO BEETHOVEN'S NINTH

Ontogeny recapitulates phylogeny.
                                                    – Ernst Heinrich Haeckel

A study was conducted recently during a woman's labor to
determine how much a baby can hear as it's being born. A
microphone by its ear revealed that the baby could easily hear
every voice in the delivery room, as well as the music playing,
Beethoven's Ninth.

1. FISH

High noon above, fish swims down so deep, can't see the sun
throwing itself like a crystal bowl against the ocean floor,
fish searching out the right spot, tail scraping across late
afternoon's lengthening shadow, hurries faster, rainbows
waving on two sides like flags of identical nations. Fish
noses under the stone, swallows the slug, lips bubble O's
against green fern, cool trickle rising through a slippery
sway of grass. She eyes a pink shell, empty as a single sigh,
one snort and the sandy ocean floor explodes, she leaps
and swerves, then down to search some more, and searches
out the spot just-so, hollows and smoothes with her pale belly
until she gets it right, fondly curls around herself, cool
as night, tail covering both her eyes, and, nestled there,
swaddled deep in red-tinged darkness, embryo.

2. LIZARD

Slow, my but she's slow, this dozer, our sister, so slow,
Sunday is Monday before you see her move. Half one thing,
half another, naked as a newt and neither egg nor fish,
this little nothing doesn't even know her name, and if
you call her, she'll never come. Just nubbins for limbs,

she's got no fingers or toes. If you're lucky, she'll
give you a wave on the ultrasound, but lacking all emotion,
she'll hold back a smile. What a nuisance, but a small one.
Lizard, slow lizard, please say your name, pretty please...

3. SNAKE

This one's all coil and rattle. When you touch her,
she moves fast as a whip in the belly, a caught spring
writhing around in the net. *Oh,* says the wife, eyes
widening, looking away from the husband, *it moved.*
What moved? her husband asks, distracted. *The baby,*
she says, *it won't stop moving.* All night she dreams
of crawling across a desert using only her arms,
dragging her swollen belly across miles of sun-
bleached sand, and when she wakes, she finds white
sheets crumpled into zigzags, like tracks across
dry sand. Snake coils, uncoils, soaks in sun
all day, cools on the crust of a rocky ledge,
and when her mother sleeps, she wakes, enacts
again her jagged circle-worship dance to the sun.

4. BIRD

Please come now pretty one, come on sweet thing to Mama,
and she's coming, in spite of herself, she's moving, head-
first, pinched like a sausage, dumb-struck with shock
and pain, hears voices and song on the other side, as,
slippery-coated with mucous, red and white and moving,
she slides toward light, letting go, letting go, head
squeezed, body wrenched, pulled thin as a string, head
crowning red, splits ragged her mother to fly, and she's
flying, open-mouthed, air-drunk, first word a howl,
as voices in unison shake white walls with song.

GOING FOR BROKE

My father gambled on failed hotels,
betting he could turn them around,
second or third hotels in Western towns
that couldn't support one. Young

as I was, I knew enough to bet
against him, putting my money
on the square called *common sense*,
as far away from the square called

heartbreak as life and the shape
of a gaming table allowed. I lost
little but time in those towns
named Shoshone and Winnemucca,

for I had my horse, Lucky, pastured
up the highway. Carrying my saddle
and bridle, I thumbed a ride to him.
Lucky and I dodged rattlers, chased

coyotes, and under a clear blue sky,
ruled our desert kingdom wisely
from our lava rock castle, while back
at the hotel, under stormy skies

of whiskey breath and Camel smoke,
old men with yellow chins pumped
their pensions into slots lining
the hotel lobby, squinted through

rheumy eyes, searching for three cherries
in blinking blue and red neon light,
and Frank, in cowboy hat and jeans,
tended bar, served 'em up straight,

winked at Evelyn, dipping into the till,
her waist cinched small by a silver belt,
and Clyde, the drunken janitor, hid
at the bottom of the basement stairs,

filling paper bags with empty wine bottles
and cat food cans he'd emptied for his meals,
while a flock of half-grown kittens, wild
as the West no longer was, yowled

in the back alley. Every night, I sat
alone at the counter in the hotel cafe,
ate my burger, fries, and chocolate shake,
then escaped the disturbance of adults,

who seemed intent on robbing one another
or being robbed. I put on my old jeans,
a long-sleeved shirt, and leather gloves,
then went to my alley hideout where,

surrounded by barrels of rancid grease,
I stalked my elusive dream: a kitten,
wild as I was, so fierce, nothing could
hurt her, tame only for me. I stuck

globs of cat food under cardboard boxes
propped up askew, but the spindly stick
broke, or the box came down crazy, and,
hissing and spitting, the kittens escaped.

Every night, I tried to trap them, but all
I ever caught was the quick and sidelong
glance of Clyde as he leered at me before
descending the steps to his dark unknown.

When my boxes came up empty, I gave in
to reality, left that greasy alley behind,
stopped trying to catch the wild cats,
relieved they'd eluded the traps.

STUCK IN THE THROAT

I couldn't cry the day my mother died.
She was shy, never good with words.

She thought that vodka made her droll.
She stored her bottles with the toilet paper.

She stuffed and zipped them into winter boots.
She hid them under Idaho potatoes.

My father drank martinis from a pitcher.
He floated olives in them, little ice.

My mother ran her car into the streetlight.
My father ran his fist into her face.

At six, I knew that secrets saved your life.
I hid the butcher knife beneath the sheets.

His hands around her neck, her face turned dark.
I meant to run the knife between his ribs.

He heard me yell, *I'm going to kill you, Daddy!*
My father knocked the knife out of my hand.

Slumped to the floor, he sobbed till dawn.
He never hit her in the face again.

The day she died, she put her make-up on.
I hoped that we could say what was unsaid.

Cancer of the throat, she couldn't speak.
We never found the words to make it right.

MADE-UP FACE

1.

In the mirror's blank stare, it takes
a long time to paint a shield
of oil and water.

2.

When the boyfriend drives up
in his '56 Chevy, she has her
make-up on, ready for the date.

Later, in his parked car,
the sheepish lipstick
slips away across his face,

the wayward pancake make-up
lolls around his shirt collar.

3.

Her face goes home with him
to his mother's knowing gaze.
He scrubs her off his skin

in the shower, his mother
tumbles her off his shirt
in the washing machine.

4.

At sixteen, in the yearbook picture,
her face is sultry,
features hidden under

sly blue eyelids,
under pancake make-up the color
of someone else's skin,

greasy weapons advertising
a dangerous desire.

COMING OF AGE IN THE FIFTIES

Under the palm trees of Southern California, the purple pompoms
of the agapanthus sway, and we high school kids believe our lives
are charmed since we outran polio on our two good legs, and after
moving to L.A. from the small-town West, Mother and I are
bombarded by daily headlines of L.A. rapes and murders, but now
we sit in movie theaters watching Marilyn Monroe and Grace Kelly
prove there's more than one way to be blonde, and later, my
boyfriend, Steve, and I don't even watch the feature because we're
kissing and petting, Steve's hand outside my dress, my nipples searching
a way through the fabric as the jacaranda tree drops its purple
trumpets to the ground. Robert Lowell names us the tranquilized
generation, while Eisenhower navigates eighteen holes, carted along by
his blank smile. Somebody always asks, *What kind of bird is singing
that song?* And somebody answers, *Mockingbird, we always say if we
don't know.* Our favorite slogan is: *Better living through chemistry,*
then, *Ha ha, how's your chemistry, Sweetheart?* yet something is being
invented every minute, and in ten years we move from ceiling fans
to air conditioning, from holding hands on the front porch of frame
houses to necking in the back seat of '55 Chevies, and my mother is the
one in four women who works, while the rest, in aqua kitchens, wear
aprons and enter favorite recipes in Pillsbury Bake-Offs, and in the
San Joaquin Valley, as migrant workers bake and pray for jobs, Steve
and I leave Pasadena on the Santa Monica freeway, speed past Venice
and Marina del Rey and El Segundo, headed toward the Lighthouse
at Hermosa Beach and the strains of West Coast jazz, where Steve will
soon play vibes with Cal Tjaeder, but for now we sit at a front table
and drink Cokes and melt into Chet Baker's voice singing, *I fall in
love too easily,* and we hold hands and walk on the beach between
sets, end up rolling around in the sand, my skirt pushed up to my
thighs, the white-haired waves falling across the sand, sighing, his leg
between my legs and we're moving, moving, while the magnolia trees
open their monstrous white blossoms and Daddy Grace preaches in
Harlem, as Negro teenagers in Little Rock pray for courage to face

the screaming mass of white faces at Central High, and flag-covered
coffins fly home from Korea, the first bad war, and McCarthy names
names, and friends of McCarthy's friends name names, and Steve
and I are kissing now, lying on the beach, his hand inside the front
of my unbuttoned dress, and Chet Baker sings, *I fall in love too fast*,
predicting he'll soon be hooked on heroin and deep in debt to the
mob, who will break his jaw, knock out his front teeth, so he can
no longer play the trumpet, and Darlene has to get married, and a
tree named the flowering paintbrush, as if startled, sheds its bristles,
which scatter like red hair across the ground, and somebody asks,
What kind of bird is singing that song? and somebody answers,
Mockingbird, we always say if we don't know, and Eisenhower
sends the 82nd Airborne Division into Little Rock to quiet the mobs
Orval Faubus stirs up, and I'm half naked now, my bra tossed
across the sand, my dress wrinkled down around my cinch belt, and
Steve asks me to go all the way, which I won't, and somewhere in
a house up the beach, three kids are twirling their Hula-Hoops in
unison, inspired by music their older sisters have put on to dance the
Bunny Hop, and I'm having my first orgasm now, the crotch of my
panties wet, as in the dark Descanso Gardens in La Cañada, roses
from 6,000 bushes release their perfume, and it's quiet there until
dawn, when 150 species of birds will serenade this dark blossoming,
and Steve tells me he can't bear it, begs me to go all the way, but I
won't, so he stands up abruptly, stares out across the waves, deep in
desperation, preparing himself for our future breakup and the heroin
overdose that will one day carry him across the whitecaps just as
he's becoming a famous musician, and Jayne Mansfield, about to
walk down the aisle to Mickey Hargitay, wears a skin-tight wedding
dress, aims her pointy breasts toward the camera, as James Dean
turns on his heel and walks away, and my mother, home alone on
a Saturday night, has by now mixed three drinks, which encourage
her to pick up the phone and try to locate my father, who's vanished
again trying to make his first million, and Mother stares into the
empty space of her life while the operator requests: *Number please?*

Number please? and Steve paces while I put on my bra, and Van Cliburn plays Tchaikovsky in Moscow, and Mrs. Billy Graham irons the Reverend's white shirt in a hotel room as he rehearses his sermon for Madison Square Garden, and Martin Luther King attends a Prayer Pilgrimage, stores up faith enough to walk him across freedom's long bridge to his death, and Gwen has to get married, and as I fasten my bra, comb my hair, and put on fresh lipstick, bougainvillea, flaming crimson, reaches for the moon.

II

Winter Heart

Northern Lights

We wait so long
for the right sky,
our prayers flying
off into space,
our eyes raised,
scanning, coming back
empty, so when it's
right, we're ready
with dry logs and
matches and help
from the sun, who takes
himself off someplace,
and help from the moon,
who hides her dear face
behind a fan of trees,
and when the sky lights
up, we tip our heads
back and give in to it,
part of us lifting off
to bathe ourselves
in light, inhale light,
become light, and we
laugh with gratitude
to be here together,
when the story could
have turned in so many
dark and varied singular
directions, here together
under a sky spinning us
a million miracles—
and, *See, there!* a fan
of white light sweeps

the sky, one minute it
shelters the whole world,
each one of us included,
the next minute it's
gone, the sky dark, no,
not quite, a few stars.

BAMBOO TRAY VARIATIONS

Sunday morning in bed,
listening to Bach, eating
a late breakfast served
on bamboo trays.

December

We feast on rolls twirled
with cinnamon and sugar—
our sweet Milky Way.

January

When you are angry,
I'll wear my silk kimono,
black, with the red sash.

February

Our bed, hostile camps.
Two spoons halt, stiffly salute,
then search our white bowls.

March

You conjure up words—
earth, water, sun—hand them to
me, poetry seeds.

April

Buds adorn branches.
From a vase, daffodils sing
above hot green tea.

May

Your hand, too large for
curved porcelain cup handles,
just right for my breast.

June

I come to your arms,
then serve strawberries, real cream,
last course of the feast.

July

The cheating lover,
tea leaves form a face in his
cup, one eye open.

August

Pitiful orphans,
wearing our grief like sunburn.
And then, the new skin.

September

One sails and one steers,
even when the wind blows hard,
holding direction.

October

Blue napkin, our tent,
beneath a full moon. Then dawn,
a thousand red birds.

November

Tree limbs, thin fingers,
point toward the sky, steadfast through
cloudy days or clear.

THREE BOYS, FIFTEEN

Body hair threatens
to grow any
moment,
        any place.

They check everything
daily, anxious
for the crop. If they
could only water and weed.

Like flocks of blackbirds
their voices scatter high
and low.
        The house reeks
of unnamed odors.

Dust floats,
        heavy,
in their rooms
waiting for a fuse,
the right match.
        Tripping
on their own music,
they lunge
        into manhood
body first.

THE CRÈCHE WARS

1.

As neighbors hang strings of colored lights, put Santas
stamped from plastic on rooftop and lawn, the five
teenagers in our almost-blended family bicker

about which crèche will grace the buffet: theirs,
housing awkward oxen and the gross baby Jesus
with his smeared red mouth, or ours, hewed to finer
lines, with delicate sheep and a dear small babe.

2.

Aesthetics being both objective and persuasive,
our side, larger by one, triumphs, and spreads
out the tableau. I swoon over the open fire
and Nat King Cole's chestnuts while the children
rudely gag and parody the folks dressed up like

Es-kee-mos. Hormones always trump harmony,
and Advent mornings dawn with adolescent shrieks
because the donkey has been found humping

Mary, or the Christ child has vanished.
I won't dignify by naming several acts the camels
are caught in. It's a long, creative season.

3.

The baby Jesus is sometimes gone for days,
or reappears at once, wrapped in swaddling clothes,
astonished to find himself under a slab of
roast pork or atop the cinnamon applesauce.

One night, four sheep wander off to graze behind
the dusty encyclopedias. They don't return until
after the crèche is boxed and stored away.

4.

Only a practical God would free-will the controversial
babe to simply disappear for good. Years later,
no one admits to know his whereabouts.

With time to grow into their new bodies, and
the manger cast dwindling, our almost-adults
renounce their Christmas vandalism, but still
mime Nat King Cole's roasting chestnuts.

Goldfish: A Small Tragedy in Four Parts

1.

Sixty years ago, I buy
two goldfish
in a glass bowl, Blackie
and Orangie,
try, at first, to keep
their water
clean, but soon forget,
I have so much
playing to do, and they
belly up,
small electrical storms
in a murky sky.

2.

Forty years ago, my sons
beg and beg for fish,
cross their hearts they'll
care for them. I hold out
for awhile, but soon give in,

so Casey and Roundhouse
begin their stay with us.
We delight in watching their
lazy trips around the bowl.
Not forgetting my past neglect,

I guide my sons, establish
a firm cleaning schedule,
which the boys, of course,
ignore, so, grumbling,
I clean the bowl myself.

In a month or two, just as
I'm tiring, Casey's tail gets
crooked and he starts swimming
sideways, while poor Roundhouse
bloats up like a balloon.

We tell ourselves it's kindness,
but, really, we can no longer
stand the sight of them, so we
flush them down the toilet,
green weeds and all.

3.

In Maui, a hostess, aspiring
to the season's most lavish
event, throws a dinner party
for fifty. Tables laden with
linen and silver, she begins
the meal with sushi, marinated
in a divine sauce, as guests
compliment the centerpieces.
Clear glass vases hold explosions
of pink proteas and purple orchids.
Inside the vases, between the cut
stems, live goldfish swim, serene
as prayers. Halfway through the
sushi, something toxic begins

to weaken the fish. One by one,
as guests freeze, forks halfway
to their mouths, the fish die,
float belly-up and catch like
cottonweed in the stems of flowers.

4.

A small Duluth restaurant,
to be more avant-garde,

supplies its diners with
goldfish, one fish circling

a wineglass in the center
of each round table.

The diners, outraged, refuse
to eat until the goldfish

are removed. Where the fish
swim off to, no one will say.

Cinnamon Applesauce

On this fuzzy-lighted fall morning, Juli, I remember when
we made applesauce—I was thirty and you were sixteen, my
kids' babysitter. Delight ruled our kitchen kingdom as chunks
of Haralson apples, held by a huge metal pan, bobbed up from
their foamy broth. We pushed them down with wooden spoons,

poured them into the Foley Food Mill and turned the handle,
forcing them through small metal holes into applesauce, which
we charmed with cinnamon and sugar, stirred by spoonfuls into
apple bubbles, burped up on the boil to the surface, the steam, the
heat, the smell transporting us to applesauce heaven.

I still remember the kitchen windows, steamed blind,
my children, who poked one another and yelled in mock
warfare, then, not getting our attention, dashed through
the kitchen, giggling, because they weren't supposed to be
in that dangerous paradise, to slip and fall in the slide

of spilled juice and sauce and sugar. Two sticky harpies,
we chased them, wooden spoons raised, laughter lifting us like
steam, as, later, the hot jars on the newspaper-covered kitchen
table popped, one by one, to the children's cries of
Ten! Eleven! Twelve! each number climaxed by cheers.

. . .

Later, you gave me jar after jar of strawberry jam, rhubarb jam,
strawberry-rhubarb jam, enough jam to charm me into a long
life. But your generosity couldn't save you. Why were you the one,
Juli, you, the one so alive, the healthy one, you with
your large breasts bobbing, breasts you never wanted,

unwilling temptress capturing the eyes of every man and boy
you passed, walking proudly, breasts held high, a burden
all your life? My younger sister, daughter, friend, why were
you the first one, in your early forties, to be pulled into your
grave by breast cancer?

. . .

Standing in front of the bathroom mirror, I look more
and more like the goddess statues at Amazon Bookstore,
no head, no arms, no legs, just two hanging breasts resting
on a bulging stomach. Should I pray to this Goddess of Breast
and Belly? Can I surrender, bow down to the mirror's
ancient truth about life and death? Should I laugh or cry?

. . .

My daughter brings me a carved match of the Virgin of Guadalupe
imprisoned in a tiny glass vial, which hangs by a cord so I can
wear her around my neck. The directions say: *First pray, then
light this match.* I can pray, Juli, but I can't burn her,
this Virgin, the beloved, I can't let her go
in a thin stream of smoke, rising...

ALL THE DEAD ANIMALS

Wearing altered forms, they greet
us as we whiz by them in our cars.
Raccoons, puffed into pillows,
deer, half gone, eaten
at night by wolves,

skunks, downed black-and-white
stripes, flag us to speed past
them holding our breath, hoping
to outrun the smell, which catches
us down the road and rides
along with us for miles.

By now, we don't mourn them,
our distant brothers and sisters,
as we do those closer to home.
The song sparrow our cat drops warm,
melody stilled, upon our bare feet.

The fierce hawk, eyes still open,
who didn't see the glass of our
picture window, and the old dog,
Uncle Harry we called him, who
was relaxing in the driveway
shadow of a pine tree

when our father drove in, sober,
blinded by the sun, and hit him.
Poor Uncle Harry, beggar that he
was, fat from all the bad food
we fed him, who followed us,

his round eyes adoring, even
when we scolded him.

Most of these animal deaths we pass
quickly, sigh, drive on through
our lives without slowing down,

but some force us to pull
over and stop. After Uncle Harry's
passing, we have a family funeral,

complete with flowers, testimonials,
and singing, before we march him
to his grave under the honeysuckle.

The hawk, stiff and cold, we hold
in our hands, enter him, eyes wide
open while we soar miles above

ourselves where we see everything
clearly, and with our altered
vision, in perspective.

Grand Portage Powwow

My favorite dancers are absent
this year—Partridge, cautiously
placing one step in front of another,

his stiff beige and brown feather
headdress bobbing up and down,

and Fox, crouching, edgy, eyes
darting back and forth, moving
soundless among the other dancers.

But this year, Black Bear has joined
the procession, his face half
blue, half black, his clothing
blue and black as well.

The other dancers make way for him
as he strides his dance, sure-footed,
smooth, taking all the room he needs.

Later, as Black Bear and I take
a break from the dancing, I meet
him at the silver jewelry stand.

Smaller than he looked dancing,
he touches the coral berries
of a necklace, first with a blue,
then with a black hand. Taking

a chance, I admire his costume,
the carefully painted figures dancing
around his arm and wristbands,
thank him for his gift.

Shy, he looks down, then proudly
tells me how difficult it was,
how long it took to paint
the right movement into the dancers.

In my mind, I see him come home
after another long day of work,
stay up late, chasing off sleep

to paint the history and power
of the tiny figures around his arms,

see him, piece by piece, become
Black Bear for one day, King
of the Forest, benevolent ruler.

WINTER HEART

Across our northern land, chickadees,
worn out from tireless labor,
have fallen asleep with their hats on.

Crows roost in groups of two or more.
Predators to young robins and songbirds,
crows are prey to Great Horned Owls,
who eat only the brains.

      . . .

The wind blows cold enough to crack,
and a December moon holds the new moon
in her arms as I once cradled my grown
son, Michael. Abhorring our wasteful

culture, he now lives his private vow
of poverty, raids dumpsters for his daily
greens, knows who discards what and when.

It's harder in winter, he says, *since fresh
things freeze so fast.* Last summer, behind
the cafe where he worked, we loaded my car

with tables and blankets left behind
by fleeing drug dealers, then drove
to Cedar Lake where he carried our cache

to the homeless camp hidden in the woods.
They'd lost the bridge they slept under
when police drilled holes so rainwater

dripped through. *Shelters aren't safe*,
he said, *especially for teenage kids.*

Today Michael carries from our house
black candlesticks made in Kenya to light
his table, a block from a crack house.

He has also taken the remains of our
holiday almonds, which he'll divide
and gift-wrap for homeless kids sleeping
in their own shelters he helped provide.

· · ·

Thousands of Alaskan moose driven
by winter's tyranny migrate to lower
land where, in search of food, over

a hundred have been hit by trains,
and so many more killed by cars,
officials have stopped counting.

· · ·

On Christmas evening, we bring sugar cookies
to our daughter, who nurses her December baby.
We watched the baby's entrance into this world,
head, as it crowned, soft as a water balloon,

then a baby girl popped out, part fish,
part bird, but fully human, formed, then painted
for her entrance with her mother's blood.

· · ·

It all depends on what the heart is able
to encompass beyond its own singular beat.

In the cold December air, hearts of sleeping
chickadees beat over 500 times a minute,

twice that when they're awake. They survive
the fiercest winter, live only a year.

. . .

In New York City, on Christmas morning,
our son, Mark, volunteers at the AIDS ward
for prisoners and the homeless. One prisoner

confides he can't celebrate Christmas.
He doesn't understand why he, of all people,
got AIDS, or why he ended up in jail.

He doesn't deserve to die; he didn't rob
that store. *I'm innocent*, he repeats.

. . .

Though the radio predicts a storm,
at this moment we can count every
star within our range of vision.

Soon it will snow again, softening
the harsh winter landscape. Some trucks
will plow, others will salt against ice.

That night, on roads cleared for our
safe passage, moose will come forth

like prehistoric dreams from deep
in the soul of the forest. While we
sleep, they will kneel to the salt.

III

The Gravity of Flesh

PICK A PRIZE

August, hot with flies, wasps
fallen sluggish to the sugar.
The State Fair, everyone eating
something or looking to be fed:
Pronto pups, chili dogs, popcorn,
cold milk, all you can drink,
Central Lutheran's homemade pie.
The woman who guesses weight,
wearing money apron and brown oxfords,
stands beside scales taller
than the big man who steps forward.
For only one pa-per dollar!
she reads his body, poundwise,
says, *Two-sixty!* He steps on
her scales at two-eighty-five.
She pats his backside under his belt
which is under a generous roll
of fat, says, *You musta' been hidin'*
somethin' there on me, honey!
Pick a prize, any prize. He touches
his thinning hair, chooses
the battered red and white beer hat
from among her ashtrays and embarrassed
lavender snakes, then walks away,
through the dusty music of calliope,
taller, twenty-five pounds lighter.

FEATHERED ATTRACTIONS

This barn is stuffed with feathers
and hundreds of caged beaks, discordant
choir of thwarted intention.
Spreading his black tattered fan
of a tail, old King Turkey gobbles,
his limp comb flopping unroyally.
Two boys holding white balloons mimic
him, when he answers back, laugh so hard
they must fall down, sitting red-faced
in the dirt aisle, then they must
roll around there, holding the white
balloons above them, the dangerous earth.
All fluffed up, a Chinese goose presses
his white chest against the bars
toward a female in the next cage.
He would force his swollen body
through the bars to her, but she
pecks her grain, seems not to notice.
On the other side of the cage, a man
catches my eye, smiles and winks, as I
turn, walk back through centuries,
each smell rousing more primitive memory,
walk back to the private room called
Women, where, alone, unobserved,
I color my lips red.

Judging Perfection

In the judging barn, 4-H finalists
kneel beside their rabbits,
pat them into soft black or tan
or white balls. Pulling up
the puffy tails, they watch the judge,
who pats and looks, then picks up
each rabbit by its ears, checking
something under there. When one
rabbit bolts, the teenage girl
covers its eyes with her hand,
and, in the dark, its rabbit brain
conjures a burrow's safety and relaxes.
The girl, overweight, her face splotched
purple and puffy, spends too much time
before her judge, the bathroom mirror.
Her thin hair will not stay out
of her eyes, her jeans will not
stay zipped. After months of hoarding
the best rabbit greens, scrubbing
the clinging ammonia smell from the cage,
ignoring algebra, the entire history
of Europe, to brush and train her pet
to as much perfection as a rabbit
will allow, a blue ribbon would help
explain such singular love.

PRETTY RICKY

He's 1200 pounds of pink pork covered by black
bristles stiff enough to needle and sew with,
Pretty Ricky, all six feet of him spread
out, asleep, no fancy dancer, neither twirler
nor prancer, just eats and sleeps, the biggest
boar at the Fair, oblivious to gawkers, smirkers,
cholesterol, or weight watchers, fat off the hoof,
fat lying flat, good only for breeding and eating,
he won't even stand to show off all the pork cuts
displayed on the poster behind him: ham, it says,
from the butt, oldest meat of civilized man;
kabobs from the shoulder, roasted on swords
by early Asian nomads; spareribs, sausage,
and bacon from the belly. Pretty Ricky urges
me to swear off pork, but it's lunchtime and my
stomach wanders off to a foot-long or a brat with
kraut. I think twice, three times, waffle back
and forth between meat and a veggie wrap, as,
in front of me, many meals stretch out, dozing.

JOINED FLESH

To the always-approaching crowd,
a man's voice announces,
They are real, human, and alive.
Straddling a single bench,
Ronnie and Donnie Galyon,
Siamese twins, they face each other
every second of their lives.
On their fifty-cent picture post card,
fastened at the waist, blue shirts pulled up
exposing their pale skin joined without a seam,
leaning back from one another, they both wave.
They enjoy hunting and fishing,
they love baseball, the Dallas Cowboy cheerleaders.
Since Ronnie wanted to learn to read,
a woman had been hired to teach them,
reading made Donnie's head ache,
when Donnie's head aches, he must lie down.
They watch television every day now.
Their trailer is air-conditioned,
people staring in through their picture window.
People staring in through their picture window,
their trailer is air-conditioned.
They watch television every day now.
When Donnie's head aches, he must lie down,
reading made Donnie's head ache.
A woman had been hired to teach them
since Ronnie wanted to learn to read.
They love baseball, the Dallas Cowboy cheerleaders,
they enjoy hunting and fishing.
Leaning back from one another, they both wave,
exposing their pale skin joined without a seam,

fastened at the waist, blue shirts pulled up
on their fifty-cent picture post card.
Every second of their lives,
Siamese twins, they face each other,
Ronnie and Donnie Galyon
straddling a single bench.
They are real, human, and alive,
a man's voice announces
to the always-approaching crowd.

Bake-off Queen

It's Marjorie Johnson! Munchkin grandma, four-foot-eight
State Fair celebrity, famous for doing what she loves best,
won 19 baking ribbons this year—7 blue and 2 sweepstakes—
one for her apple pie, adding up to 2500 ribbons during
her 32-year Fair career, started baking at 8 and she's
never stopped, *Oh brother!* how fast she talks, takes
notes on everything she bakes just like an experiment,
makes a chart, always tries to improve, *Oh my gosh!* she's
been on Jay Leno with uploads to YouTube, for years she
entered the fair in 70 categories, didn't enter cookies
this year—only 25 categories allowed now—*Oh brother!*
a hard choice, always wears a red dress, drip-dry, shows
up well on TV, rinses it out at night, hangs it over the
tub to dry, *Oh my gosh!* she's one of a kind! Best of show!

THE MIDWAY

Tom's Alpine Train ride, fueled
on gasoline and screams, climbs up up up
its two-railed Alps,
coasts down again, that crazy clackety-clack.
The young couples,
their constant touching, making sure the one
they've found is still there,
the children, reciting their alphabets of terror,
and others, feeling old,
trying to remember their first time
with fear a new acquaintance.
Tom wears reflecting mirror glasses, silver,
white T-shirt,
sleeves rolled high displaying more muscles
than should fit
around any arm, and a blue Hawaiian girl tattoo,
her torso twitching
when his muscles move her this way and that.
Tom tells his folks
to trust him, he'll never let them down,
he'll take them
the whole way up the Alps, grinning
as they scream
on up, grinning as they scream on down, and Tom,
his eyes his own
secret, talking them through, talking them.

The Horticulture Building

So many orchids,
we sail abroad, tropically
seduced by color.

. . .

Bonsai trees assume
athletic poses, twisting
this way and that. Wrapped,

then wired to thwart growth,
they remain the small shadows
of gigantic trees.

. . .

Color and perfume,
orchids cast their charms on us
and we can't resist.

First-time Fairgoers

Parking the stroller that holds
her plump son, the woman
newly arrived from Viet Nam
stops at the hawker's stand.

She does not touch
the American flag, small,
on a stick, not the pennant
announcing *Minnesota* in gold
and maroon, not even pink balloons.

What she touches is the tray
of plastic bird whistles, fingers
the blue warbler, the yellow,
the red. Choosing a yellow canary,
she hands the man her money.

The hawker rests his cigar stump,
and blows warbles flying
through the humid August air,
then gives the whistle to her,
refusing the money.

The small woman, in black-wrapped
skirt and T-shirt, laughs with her
entire body, laughs, leaning over,

warbling for her round-faced boy,
who laughs and slaps his hands
on the shiny stroller.

When she gives him the whistle,
too young to make a song,
he flies the yellow warbler
through thin air. The hawker

picks up the whistle, returns it to her,
then bows from the waist, goodwill
ambassador whose perfect action
changes nothing but this moment.

Hawkers Et Cetera

They're all selling something, yellow chamois towels, $21
for two, use them to pick up spills, dry after a bath, or
chamois your car, don't be shy, step right up and touch
this amazing new invention! After you use it on your car,
wash it in bleach to kill the germs, then dry your dishes,

and don't forget one of these Welcome Signs for your home,
propellers, wind-driven, the spinning propeller turns the
tractor wheels, helps the horse and cowboy lasso the bull,
the hunter shoot the duck, the full martini glasses tip
your way with the saying, "It's 5 o'clock somewhere!"

and the Ginsu knives that cut tomatoes like butter, these
knives are so sharp you can even shave the eyelashes off
a mosquito, yes, folks, you don't need sharp words or sharp
looks, but you do need sharp knives, serrated so they never

need sharpening, plus slicers, peelers, butterflyers,
scallopers, all with a surgical, stainless steel edge and
fifty-year guarantee, want your slices flower-shaped?
use this spiral slicer, down and down, around and around,

make your friends jealous when you cut a beautiful garnish
for your table, Voilà! Didn't know I spoke French did ya'?
and right now for you early birds, I'm authorized to cut
the price in half, I said, in half, one set for just $99,

and Custom-Made Shoes and Boots from Charlotte, North
Carolina, made in Quito, Ecuador, just come forward, step on
this piece of paper, and we'll take your footprint for a
measure, it's as easy as that, Ostrich at $600, Elephant at

$650, Sting-Ray at $890, and Alligator for $990! Look at these Alligator boots taken from four different places on that old gator, the sides, the top, the toe, and the back, just place your foot on the paper, then place your order, and soon you'll be struttin' your stuff all over town!

THE BOND OF FLESH

A motorcycle stunt man rides
his circle in the air
while a woman dangles under him,
circling in this unnatural orbit
of motor and machine.
She hangs first by her toes,
arms outstretched toward her
distant grave, and then by her teeth,
one toe pointed, ladylike, upon
her moving knee. How lightly he steers
the loud machine on its road
of metal rope. Around they go,
picking up speed until the crowd
responds with movement and noise,
clapping, then cheering. Heads tipped
back, a couple stands, watching.
The man's knuckles are red
where he has scrubbed
with a brush, but 10-40 oil
still lines the fold and curve
of his strong fingers. He rests
his arm around his wife's
shoulders. She relaxes, laughing,
as she leans on him, forgetting
to hide her bad teeth.

REVELATION

Three Mexican women, dark stars
of the Aerial Thrill Circus, rise
high above the crowd. Lifted up
by their heads and La Cucaracha,
they take off their teal-blue dresses,
stripping down to silver sequins,
bare legs, bare shoulders and backs,
as the crowd cheers on this near
revelation. Three dresses fall
slowly, silken feathers from beyond
where we can run or jump,
as the silver women, alone in the sky,
submit again to the universal spin, faster
and faster, their bodies blur
into motion and light, then slow
and descend again, epistles written
within their shining bodies
and delivered back to earth by these
devout children of the innocent air,
who will never tell us what
they have learned, except to say,
by example, that it can be done.

IV

What the Eyes Must See

WHAT THE EYES MUST SEE

1.

We live our lives with eyes
half closed. What's to be gained
from the feather-fine inspection
of a songbird glued to the road
by its own guts, flesh trucked
away above the scurry of ants,
or the close scrutiny that
reveals how deprivation drains
the skin of color, scars the face
of a drunk? We know that under
the lush veneer of the painted
virgin, coyly posed, programmed
into canvas is the death mask
of the widow who bore her, know
the cathedral's vault can
only approximate the arch
of sky, and though the cross
hangs free of its risen corpse,
each day we live, hundreds
are hung to drip their lives
away beyond our horrified gaze.
So what's to be gained by
fixing our eyes on the turned-
over cup of wine, crimson stain
expanding, when only moments
before, the cup was full and red
as a pomegranate, split open
to offer up its chorus of seeds?

2.

With eyes half closed, we cannot
see that the mission nearby
lacks food to nourish the drunk,
whose scripture is red wine,
so he can live to pray again.
And, if we're dozing, how can
we write out checks to those who
stand up, unarmed, for the fragile
song of a bird against jungle
bulldozers? Both widows and virgins
hang on crosses they had no part
in carving, and we know that rivers
carry their burden of blood
in many nations where laws obey
the largest gun. Even the church
offers no sanctuary against bombs,
and ignorance is seldom defeated
while kneeling. If, without thought,
we devour the entire pomegranate,
lush and moist before us, what
seeds will remain for the planting?
Who will harvest, who will eat?

WITNESSES: OCTOBER 1996

1.

Somewhere in Rwanda, a Tutsi
woman sits alone in an empty
room watching the Hutu refugees
return from their camp in Goma,

Zaire. She wears a simple dress
wrapped around her stiff body;
she wears a permanent machete
scar wedged between her eyes.

Any moment now, those men who
two years ago killed her husband,
her five children may pass
before her. She will know them
when she sees them.

2.

As she watches, another Tutsi,
a man, works in the fields
trying to bury his sorrow.

He has not returned to his home
for two years. Among the half-
million Hutus returning are those

who killed his grandparents,
parents, aunts, uncles, cousins,
and the children, the children.

As the Tutsi man moves dry dirt
around in circles, the killers
move into his former home where
generations of memories drained

into the earth with only flies
to witness. Flies can sing,
they can even dance, but they
cannot testify, nor can they tell
the ancient family stories.

Returning from the fields,
this man meets the story killers.
He greets them politely
as is the way in his village.

Hello, he says, bowing his head
toward them. *Hello*, they say,
bowing in return. From this day

forward, the killers will sit
on his chairs, light his lamps,
lie down on his bed.

3.

This Tutsi man and woman want
justice done, but so many dead,
so many killers. Justice just

wants to lie down and sleep.
Someone wants to keep her
awake; someone wants to buy
her a soft bed, satin pajamas.

Hutu refugees walk for days
without food. Little boys strip
fat stalks of sugarcane with
their teeth. The Red Cross

supplies twenty high-energy
biscuits that must last for
three days. The refugees shuffle
past by the tens, hundreds,

thousands, as somewhere in
Rwanda a man walks past his
occupied home, and the refugees

keep coming, as a woman sits
alone in an empty room watching
them return from their camp

 in Goma, Zaire. Her head aches
 behind the scar she has been
given, but she does not stop
watching. This watching

from an empty room, this dream
that justice will not lie
down and fall asleep is all
she has left of her life.

Contour Line Drawing

Our thumbs the first model, we move
a pen around them on the page,
really seeing for the first time

knuckle hills, the plowed furrows
stretched across them, white half-
moons shining above thumbnail

skies, our finished work ancient
as the first hands drawn centuries
ago on a cave wall by firelight.

After the hijacked plane crashed
in the reaped field, they found
two hands bound at the wrists.

Now we draw our whole hand lying
on its back, curled fingers reaching
toward us, as in sleep or death.

Two people jumped from the flaming
towers, cartwheeled all the way down
through smoke and ash holding hands.

We trace the second finger pointing
toward the unknown, try to catch
the palm's curve, its maze of destiny.

Next we trace the lifeline, its deep
groove dark in the innocent hand,
the line a palm reader measures

to gladly announce a long life ahead,
or looks down to mask her expression
for a lesser truth than what she sees.

The chef, a hundred floors up, chopped
beets, the window washer squeegeed,
and a broker wrote in her day planner

as they took their secrets with them,
their delights and lies, failures
and dreams, years they hadn't lived.

Those who were lost return to dwell
in the negative space between our fingers,
their faces barely imprinted on our palms,

cupped to hold treasure we took for granted
until it was so lost that even our hands
holding photographs couldn't find it.

After Breast Cancer

The resident with an accent
thought I was anxious
because I asked questions.

Cancer answers one question:
*What will you do with the next
few years of your life?*

It proves how powerful
the unseen can be, ushers out
any illusion you will live

forever, ushers in pain, nausea,
unending sleep. It speaks
through your body about war:

*Cancer cells are programmed
to multiply, travel, and destroy.*

Doctors and their platoons
of armed soldiers hunt them
down, take no prisoners.

Radiation wounds every cell
it attacks. Only healthy cells
can repair themselves:

*Cancer cells are programmed
to multiply, travel, and destroy.*

The resident from another
country thought I was anxious
because I asked questions

even though I just wanted
to understand. Perhaps women
from his country don't ask

questions, perhaps he thinks
older women are anxious. Twice,
he said, *Miss Breckenridge, there*

is no cancer in your entire body.
I refrained from asking,
Can you promise me that?

Cancer cells are programmed
to multiply, travel, and destroy.

THREE SURGERIES LATER

When I woke from ignorant
sleep, I'd been robbed,

left with the living room
trashed, one lamp broken,

a window forced open.
They didn't take every-

thing I owned, took only
the tall silver coffee pot

holding the largest portion,
took the round silver tray

that all else rests upon.
Luckily, they overlooked

the squat teapot of my
silver tea service, left

me with the promise of tea,
that heals most afflictions,

tea that steeps an aromatic
brew I share with friends,

left me the matched sugar and
cream set. Sugar and cream

to sweeten my remaining days,
circled by the human treasure

they didn't steal, those still
living and those in memory.

V

Light, Wings, Hand

LIGHT, WINGS, HAND

Caught in blinding rain,
I clutch the steering wheel,

narrow my eyes to slits,
drive slowly to my cabin

where a flutter of wings
surround the porch light,

too many wings to count.
When I unlock my door,

light and wings that
beckoned the way escort me

into waiting darkness.
This morning, only one

moth silhouette remains
in my bathroom sink, white

porcelain wings outlined
by powdered brushstrokes

of beige, empty inside
the lines like a childhood

drawing of a hand after
the child is grown, gone

but not gone like those
wings washed down my drain,

like the porch light, long
forgotten, guiding me home.

Birthday Haircut

Above the Mississippi River
on its slow roll to the sea,
our electric clippers buzz
as I cut hair on the porch.

He's just announced he'll
remain sixty-seven—that's close
enough to seventy, thank you.
He won't lie, really, just say

his chosen age along with the real
one, fancy set slightly before fact.
The ponytail at the nape of his
neck grows thinner every year.

Not enough hair to worry about
on top, so I clip the curly fuzz
on the back of his neck, clumps
I can't catch flying from

the fifth floor into May's hands
who will present it, perhaps,
to the rosy finch, wearing
his hooded red cape, who warbles

mornings from our porch railing.
Spring, where one familiar thing
becomes another—brown branches
soften into green, green buds flare

into yellow, lavender, and pink,
love becomes haircut on a warm
morning in the middle of May,
cut hair becomes lining for

silent cups that will soon fill
with naked cries for food, cries
quieted for a moment with what
little comfort love can bring.

BEER BARREL POLKA

Rising from the parking lot by Lake
Superior's beach, floating up between
gold and red leaves of birch and maple,
the accordion strains of "Beer Barrel
Polka." How I hated practicing that
song when I was nine, hated strolling

among guests in my black taffeta skirt
and white satin blouse playing "Beer Barrel
Polka," the number I got the most requests
for at my parents' drunken parties,

rooms hazed with cigarette smoke,
glasses in every hand; then "Tea for Two,"
the toothy gushing of women, scarlet
lipstick smeared across their teeth;
then "Ghost Riders in the Sky," men's sly
looks, pinches, slack whiskey grins

while I walked among them, a grim smile
pasted on my lips, as doomed as they
were, doing my time, serving my sentence
until I could make an escape, my right

hand stretched across the white keys,
my left hand pounding the bass notes
as the bellows hissed, opened and closed,
opened and closed, and I, a snotty
little Cinderella, belted it out.

Now, from the beach, laughter echoes
up the hill with that jolly beer hall tune,
laughter mixed with blinding sunlight
and the sound of waves as people pile out
of the car singing those stupid words, *Roll
out the barrel, we'll have a barrel of fun!*

and dance around the accordion player.
While red and gold leaves fall among them,
they shed for a moment their failures
and disappointments as the accordion
squeezes a bit of delight from this cold

lemon of a world, and the awkward dancers,
tossed into a crazy circle by the song,
throw their heads back, wrap their arms
around each other and reach for the reprieve

of laughter, stumble toward the fleeting
pardon of joy, like my hapless parents
those many years ago, they and their sodden
friends long gone, all of us doomed, all
of us pardoned, all of us free at last.

PRUNING THE GERANIUMS

On the first day of autumn,
arriving at our little cabin
after a week's absence,
I prune the geraniums, pluck

crusty brown centers from
blossoms, throw them onto
the pre-frost green grass.

   ...

Since my right hip
was replaced with titanium,
it makes the airport
security guards crazy.

They hover around me
like demented fairy
godmothers, their magic
wands screeching.

   ...

I snap off the withered
blooms where they join
the main stem, toss
them away—others still

hold a cluster of small
buds hanging under
the main flowers.

After they turn rusty,
more buds open, putting

forth every bit of
pink they possess.

   ...

In the bath, a red scar,
ten inches long, shouts
out from my hip.

When I was in the hospital,
nurses told me that
the operating room before
a hip replacement looks

like a mechanics shop
with its retinue of saws,
hammers, and chisels.

They said no other surgery
bleeds more. Later I realized
they nearly cut off my leg.

New joint in place, they
stapled shut the jagged wound.
 When I could walk again, metal
staples puckered my skin.

   ...

While I was in the city,
Scruffy, the old doe,
dined on our edible flowers.

Partial to petunias,
she doesn't refuse pansies.
So far, the geraniums
are safe. I don't begrudge

her animal nature
since last summer she lost
one fawn, then the other

on the highway as they
crossed from the forest
to drink in Lake Superior.

Scruffy's muzzle has turned
gray. She probably won't
bear many more fawns.

        ...

When I was younger, old
people told me that after
the body ages, the heart
still feels young.

It's true. Although my body
limps along, something within
me feels light and joyful
as a tiny bird at dawn.

        ...

I've read that just before
harvest, even on the darkest
nights, the ripe corn, full

kernels pushing against
their husks, glows. Glows
even without a full moon.

I have never seen this,
but I know it must be true.

PEACE

'Tis peace of mind...
we must find.

– Theocritis

Peace is not an absence
but a presence. In Liberia,
peace of mind means, *My*
heart sits down. Other

Africans call peace of mind
A body song, or *Where*
the cool water runs.

Peace is an act of doing,
an act of doing we keep
on doing, we keep on

singing our body song
where the cool water runs
as our heart sits down

in the presence of light,
our gift of song rising.

LUCKY LOVE

Oh, lucky to be loved,
lucky to have the hand
of your lover on your hand,
lucky to have the lover's hand
on your brow, on your breast,
on your heart, oh, the heart
that heals even the deepest
hurt, the heart that knows
how lucky it is to love,
then love some more, even
when there's nothing much left
to love, the love still flows,
this love that lives on
beyond the last breath,
oh, lucky to be loved.

QUESTIONS AND ANSWERS

So much of childhood is spent
in a manner of waiting,
the future mysterious

as the infinite clouds rolling
away to hidden destinations,
and so much of old age is spent

in a manner of wondering,
asking all the questions
that don't have answers:

How much longer do I have?
Will I have enough money?
Will I suffer or be alone?

Asking the questions, then
letting them go, trying to
let them go, then letting

them go, for all you can
do is walk across the ice
that may be too thin

to hold, but you keep
walking, just keep walking,
and then you notice

the sky, how it's never been
exactly that shade of blue,
the clouds forming into shapes

your imagination plays around
just like you did in childhood
when you were waiting.

THE BLACK AND WHITE HORSE

Walking deep in the woods, I search
for healing herbs, look for the balm
only forest green can provide.

As sunlight struggles to break through
a cover of dark clouds, leaves rustle,
whisper secrets to a warm wind.

A young man leading a fine horse
steps from the forest and

approaches me. The horse is piebald,
black and white. Unsaddled, he prances
on tiny hooves, wants to run.

The man gives me a beguiling smile,
offers me the piebald horse with his
long neck, his small head, like hunting

horses in old English paintings, legs
stretched out far in front and behind.

The man leaves me alone with the horse,
who snorts, still wants to run. How

will I ride this wild young horse?
I have no saddle, I am old, fearful,

until I see the man again across
the dense woods, too far away to call.

I know he is still smiling, hear him,
although it is silent, speak to me:

I have given you the horse of darkness
and light. He can run faster than
fear itself. When your heart has

emptied of all it has to give, climb
on his back. He will run, stretch out
to his full length and carry you across.

NOTES

Page 6: "Evolution and Birth to Beethoven's Ninth" – For Deborah Keenan and her (then) baby, Cordelia Siedel.

Page 19: "Northern Lights" - For Chad Haldeman and Alexia Chrisan

Page 30: "Cinnamon Applesauce" – For Juli Mantor

Page 32: "All the Dead Animals" - For Linda Wing

Page 36: "Winter Heart" – For Mike Haldeman, Mark Haldeman, Sharon Fenn, and Madeline Fenn

Page 47: "Bake-Off Queen" is a Found Poem, much of it taken from the article, "Oh My Gosh!" by Kim Ode in the *StarTribune*, September 3, 2007.

Page 61: "Witnesses: October 1996"

In 1994, in the Central African Republic of Rwanda, Hutu militia massacred as many as one million Tutsis in a state-sanctioned genocide. Later, many Hutus fearing retaliation fled to Zaire, where they lived in refugee camps supported by the world community.

In October 1996, Tutsi rebels fought and defeated the Zairian military in East Zaire. Over a million Hutu refugees deprived of food and protection began to starve, then walked by the thousands in a mass migration back to Rwanda.

Page 79: "Pruning the Geraniums" – for Sharon Chmielarz

Page 82: "Peace" - Phrases from a *Days of Healing—Days of Joy* meditation for January 10, by Earnie Larsen and Carol Larsen Hagarty, published by Hazelden, 1987,1992.

Page 83: "Lucky Love" - Thanks to Gerald Stern and his poem, "Lucky Life."

INDEX OF TITLES

About the Author

photo by Jackie Oderman

Jill Breckenridge grew up in the West, but now lives and writes in Minneapolis, Minnesota. She and playwright John Fenn raised a combined family of five children together. Jill works as an editor, focusing on both writing product and process. A former Director of the Loft Literary Center, she originated The Mentor Series, a program connecting national and local writers.

Jill won The Bluestem Award, judged by William Stafford, for her book of poems, *How To Be Lucky*. Her sequence of poetry and prose about the Civil War, *Civil Blood*, was published by Milkweed Editions. The book was nominated for the American Library Association's Notable Books of 1986. Jill's honors include a Bush Foundation Fellowship, two Minnesota State Arts Board grants, and Loft-McKnight Awards in both poetry and prose.

Her poems have appeared in many publications, and are anthologized in *Minnesota Writes: Poetry*; *25 Minnesota Poets*; *Woman Poet: Midwest*; *Looking for Home: Women Writing about Exile*; *Family Reunion: Poems about Parenting Grown Children*; *To Sing Along The Way: Minnesota Women Poets from Pre-Territorial Days to the Present*; and *Where One Voice Ends Another Begins: 150 Years of Minnesota Poetry*.

Jill holds an MFA in Creative Writing and a Master's Degree in Counseling Psychology, with an emphasis on creativity. Her website is ***www.JillBreckenridge.com.***